The Pain Trader

The Pain Trader

and Other Poems

by

James Fowler

Golden Antelope Press
715 E. McPherson
Kirksville, Missouri 63501
2020

ISBN: 978-1-936135-89-9 (1-936135-89-2)

Library of Congress Control Number: 2020932421

Published by:
Golden Antelope Press
715 E. McPherson
Kirksville, Missouri 63501

Available at:
Golden Antelope Press
715 E. McPherson
Kirksville, Missouri, 63501
Phone: (660) 665-0273
http://www.goldenantelope.com
Email: ndelmoni@gmail.com

Contents

CONTENTS

Acknowledgments:

- *Aji Magazine*: "Revelation"

- *Along the River*: "Brown Study in Blue and Gray"; "Caving"

- *Cave Region Review*: "A Day at the Races"; "Below, Above"; "County Museum"; "Eureka"; "Gayne Preller Takes Stock"; "Insider"; "IQ Zoo"; "Mountain Airs"; "Original Sin"; "Ouachita Wonderland"; "Pearl"; "The Pioneers"; "A Psalm of Ed"; "Refugees from Atlantis Wash Ashore in Northwest Arkansas"; "The Striper"

- *Elder Mountain*: "Arc"; "Over Here"; "Ozark Yarn"; "The Pain Trader"; "Sundown"

- *Futures Trading Magazine*: "Exegesis"

- *Intégrité*: "Goat" (forthcoming)

- *Out of Our*: "Imitation of Christ"

- *Poetry Quarterly*: "Forecast"

- *Star*Line*: "Sci-Fi in Midsummer South"

- *Valley Voices*: "Cabin Fever"; "Natchez"

Preface

This collection is divided into two parts, "Hereabouts" and "Thereabouts." The first part, set in Arkansas, roughly cycles from past to present, while also moving north to south. Though the organization in the second part is looser, it also has something of an historic arc, while ranging throughout the South.

The Arkansas poems draw on such sources as *The Encyclopedia of Arkansas*; Joe David Rice's *Arkansas Backstories*; Steven and Ray Hanley's *Main Street Arkansas*; various articles in the *Arkansas Democrat-Gazette*; exhibits at Crystal Bridges Museum, the Old State House Museum, the Historic Arkansas Museum, and several country museums; and my travels around the state. In a dozen or so poems, I decided that a contextual note might be helpful for some readers. Poems with notes each end with an asterisk; notes are at the end of the book.

I would like to thank the journal editors who have previously published some of the poems in this volume, especially Tim Coone (*Cave Region Review*), Phillip Howerton and Craig Albin (*Elder Mountain: A Journal of Ozarks Studies*), John J. Han (*Intégrité*), and John Zheng (*Valley Voices: A Literary Review*). The English Department at the University of Central Arkansas has for many years encouraged my creative as well as scholarly works. I am also grateful to Betsy and Neal Delmonico, editors of Golden Antelope Press, for generously bringing this whole project to fruition.

Finally, I dedicate this volume to my mother and late stepfather, for their unwavering support of my literary pursuits.

Hereabouts

The Pioneers

Shape the place to their liking,
making inroads on wilderness.
The wolves howl in protest
but slip through the forest.

Trappers decked in eight animals
define frontier fashion;
boasting through beards,
they reel with knives flashing.

The surplus of many things—
elms, trout, and red men—
calls for prodigal management,
a westward spring cleaning.

So they smooth-talk the flinty tribes
and strong-arm the marshy
to pack up their buffaloes
and hunker on barrens.

They are besting the beavers,
harassing the poison oak,
importing wallpaper with
scenes chaste and idyllic.

The bells in their steeples
ring righteous entitlement,
the hoo-ha of ownership
raised up like hosannas.

It's a tale of conversion,
from raw stuff to barrelhead,

first tapping of maples
then sweets underground.

A destined dominion lies
in pushing to margins,
as though filling an emptiness
while covering tracks.

Revelation

Eight days out of Arkansas Post
and he'd seen nary a one, white or red.
Just himself and woodland creatures.
Wasn't that what drew him at first,
not long after the Purchase, the chance
to settle ahead of the crowd?
So now these wild stretches, hill
and hollow, were practically his alone.
Unaware, he fingered Heckaton's amulet,
a charm for good hunting. If only
it all weren't so desperate.
He needed a rare thing of Nature,
a white deer, to counter a poison
dire and outlandish in its action.
He wouldn't end like that boy
in Kentucky, lashed to a bed frame,
frothing and snapping. Beforehand,
he would make peace on his terms.

By the eleventh day he'd spotted
several bucks, grand antlered sovereigns,
and would have shot one otherwise.
As it was, he stuck to small game,
moving meal to meal. Once he had to
persuade a black bear to forage
for its own dinner. The weather was cold,
but no snow had denned animals yet.
Still, trekking all day as he did,
he sometimes felt heated, partly from
having to keep the worry under.
He also tamped down the word *feverish*.

When swooped by a jay, he dove
to the ground and cursed himself
for a coward, spooked by winged things
that bite. Out night hunting, he'd found
himself the prey. Two small drops
of blood wrenched him loose from life.
Folks said he had a month, maybe two,
to track down a bezoar more precious
than diamonds.

                    In his third week
he stood on a height looking east,
to where the river ribboned through
the dense growth. At first he thought
himself a touch wobbly from the climb,
but then the ground seemed in motion,
rippling in waves like a woman shaking
crumbs from a tablecloth. And like waves
on the shore, they broke in spray,
steamy disgorgings from the depths.
He'd heard that the poison did this,
made the stricken imagine things,
unreal things. For want of a madstone,
he might need cross into madness.
If so, it was coming on hard, as he
now saw trees walking like men
in ranks downhill. Not a praying body,
he was forced to his knees,
and held his head for very sanity.
Birds swirled above by the thousands,
and in the river below a shape
arose to push against the stream.

Verses of Scripture drilled into him
when young, a chronicle of end times,
played out before his astonished gaze.
A whole mass of forest to the south
simply sank from view. Likewise,
his own small fear for his skin
that had driven him to this place
was swallowed up by a larger,
an awe that cauterized all wounds.

The hours and days that followed,
racked with slippages and tremblings,
showed the world itself convulsed,
not him. He would turn home.
Most beasts had fled the wreckage.
On a distant ridge he even saw
a Cherokee band beat a path westward.
Somehow he thought a man who lived
to tell such a tale would live.
Hardly the preaching kind, he could yet
bear witness to wonders in the earth
vouchsafed a lone wanderer, now set
on gaining himself a wife and child.*

The Pain Trader

Works in horn, wood, bone.
Itinerant, he appears in the yard,
asking for water; tells of pigeons
on the wing, nations of bison.

Shortly his talk gives way to
quiet, hands abstractly busy
as folk hear themselves unpack
their sorry load of troubles:

Failed crop, marriage, business,
all so singular and hard,
like a child named and buried,
raw cicatrix of loss.

They'd rather not hold it
against the world, try to strike
the right accepting tone,
but it's hard. The hurt burrows.

All this while a shape emerges,
carved, etched: creaturely perhaps;
blossoming; stark like crystals.
A thing of power rough hewn.

They see and know it theirs
at some remove, not so particular
as first felt, a more broadly
veined and grained likeness.

So they barter, setting shrewdness
aside, surprised what value
something neither finery nor tool
can have by their reckoning.

Arkopolis

A city on hills beside a river,
wilderness at first supplying logs
for shelter, then planks for framing
more proper houses with painted fronts,
lines of them on named lanes,
in their midst a district for trade,
eventually faced with brick and stone,
rising higher above paving and nervous
ganglia of wires strung insistently like
a gathering purse seine for people.
The needful dilates, from general store
and saloon to jail and opera house.
Here at the destined crossing—
southwest by land, southeast by water—
culture rises from modest stakes
in hogs and bowie knives to crowning
institutes: a laboratory for democracy,
a museum of overlooked wonders,
The Fraternal Order of Reformed Merchants.
Here the classics are translated into
Cherokee and Mandarin; schoolchildren stage
the byways of history unrolling to
crayon dioramas; ministers preach with
the accuracy of scholars; and scholars write
with demotic zest and Attic salt.
In short, the future takes its contours
from prior rings, as nature corridors
with deer and fox thread the latest
engineering feats, and night creatures peruse
nearby sculpture gardens after hours.

Here wood and stream are never far
to seek. The violin and fiddle lie down
together in this peaceable kingdom.
Quilts soften the athenaeum walls.
Laughter ripples the chautauqua tent.*

Below, Above

Word spreads: not coal, but salt, lead.
There for the chipping. Also caves.
With bats. Bats above, guano below.
Stuff for gunpowder. Salt of the earth.
Gunpowder and lead, a natural armory.

Or fertilizer, if so inclined.
Among all this upheaval, flat stretches
for shack and garden, a fruiting tree perhaps.

Several generations later, a proper house
and commercial orchard. One of many.
Much not of the best, but good enough
for cider and jack, flourishing until
nation's Northwest outgrows state's.

Scattered remnants now.
But picture beside a twisty route
a sudden stand: Arkansas Black,
heritage, unhybridized further.
Plunk down a dollar.
Polish on jeans.
Dig in.

Aftermath

—the *Sultana* disaster

Nathan seen it first, that first body
driftin' downstream just after sunup.
Wasn't nothin' new, specially in spring flood.
Then come a dead mule, then a horse,
then a couple more Feds. We knew
Bobby Lee'd folded his hand a few weeks
back, and thought maybe bushwhackers
was gettin' in some last licks.
Then Jeb called from a patch of shore
trees with water ten foot up their trunks.
It was tangled in the branches, so we
fished it out with poles from
Ole Man Jenkins' raft. "Goddam,"
Jeb muttered, "this Yank died hard."
He was part burnt, and a mite swole,
with a rag of bandage over one eye.
Not to be outdid, Nathan nudged me
and pointed midstream, where a clump
of blue and river trash whirled past.
We couldn't quite reckon it, till
Jeb slapped his leg and declared,
"That steamer yestiddy mornin',
packed to the rails and sorta leanin'
round the bend." Hit like gospel truth.

Maybe right after Vicksburg fell
we might of whooped and seed
the hand of Providence payin' out.
But now when nothin' but thorns

is reaped, and bullet for bullet
stretches murder out to kill
peace itself, a floatin' charnel house
like this don't count for good.
Must be all that death ain't quite
draint out of the works just yet.*

Over Here

We come here to be shut of all that,
settled into hills and minded our business,
maybe partial to blood feuds,
but not such as drag whole countries in.
Our own hands worked this ground,
never bound another to it, the way
they done in the lowlands,
them with their po-faced lost cause
spread like a rash these thirty year.
Outsiders say we're as flinty as
our cliffs, backward as a mule rump.
And now we up and refused their war,
they call us chicken thieves, slackers,
socialists and wild-eyed Russellites.
Be that as may be, we'll not be made
to muck in Europe's slop like penned hogs.
So if Mr. Wilson sees fit to send
militias in an appeal to reason,
they'd best beware: we can melt
into thickets thicker than their skulls
and snipe with the best.
Never no more will boy hereabouts
kill his own self before being shamed
into killing some like foreign soul.
So come, all you deputized fools,
step into our cove's finished mystery
and repent your war with mountain folk.*

Sundown

Off the books, so hard to nail down,
except that sign at town's edge

No malaria, no loose dogs, no. . . .

Unreconstructed, it buzzes at sawmill,
puckers like vinegar from bad apples

A second chance to fly the flag,
join the brotherhood that rides by night

No malaria, no loose dogs, no. . . .

Hit the trail, it snarls, the road
paved with disinfections

Yours the boondocks, the rough precincts,
ours the share we will not share

You have until—don't let us find—
we won't be held responsible

*No malaria, no loose dogs, no. . . .**

Arc

Scattered clapboard stores with porches
at first, something to justify a name:
Hoxie, Mountain Home, Calico Rock, Lead Hill.
Maybe tracks to align beside, a nearby
stream. Intentions are firmed with brick,
blocks squared off, to set flivvers
lurching into town over washboard roads
for big 20¢ meals, the latest in notions.
Eventually stray pigs and hens
decamp for the boondocks, their kind
best seen dressed for Sunday supper.
It's a self-respecting place now,
electrified, plumbed, paved curb to curb.
The four-sided bank clock at
First and Main declares there's no
bad time for business (one write-off
decade aside). Comes the heyday of
Ben Franklin, Rexall, Western Auto,
parades anchored by the Fighting Panthers.
But then the slow march of vacancy,
as dollars find other roosts. At best,
abstract replaces concrete: title office, dry goods.
Townsfolk plot improvement districts,
finally give arts the time of day.
With luck or pluck full circle
could simply mean a weedy lull
before this enterprise's second whirl.

Mountain Airs

I: Homecoming

Wouldn't die
without seeing Europe.
Saw it and lived:
moon wallow,
potter's field,
banquet for rats.

Came home and lived
through influenza.
Found remedy
in morning fogs,
creature calls,
walking the mountain
in many weathers.

Came home and married
a girl from school
he never fancied
but now found
likely.

She'd looked for more
but gratified
his second asking.

II: Settling

She has her father's violin
for keeping, just for keeping,
and his pocket classics in
their worn leather skins.

Once he lived in Boston
before freefalling times
brought him to meager
Ozark village barter.

Now she in turn learns
isolated mountain ways
with a cloudy man
most at home in silence

as a boy at heels wants
all she knows on lions.
Come sunset there's a breeze
and Robert's dobro waxes sweet.

The strains of joy and sorrow
don't part too readily
is what the music says
and what her days repeat.

III: What He Recalls about His Second Child's Birth

The doctor arrived in a chariot of fire,
a wonder on wheels made in Little Rock.

Its oversized tires, its oversized everything
enchanted and awed him together.

A Climber for sure, a yellow behemoth
for conquering washouts and ruts in style.

Just picture it rumbling on stumps, on shale,
taking the top of the mountain by storm.

Not normally given to envy, he thinks
it a lesser man's summons to larceny.

Such as himself must fall back on the line
of angling for heavenly blue tipped with green.

***

From the bed his deflated mate held up
a puckered tomato airing its griefs.

IV: Clara's Vision

They're under down south
in the great delta lake,
out of their depth,
over their houses.

Depressions cross the sky,
soaking the poor
on their bottomlands.

This rain that pours
pours in dust
and pours in locusts
and pours in soup.

Though perched on high
she feels the flood,
the drying jobs,
the drowning debt.

Seldom less than hard,
now a sight harder.
A use for every scrap,
and a second, then another.

Tacked to her wall
the Taj Mahal,
tribute to a woman
after she's gone.

Some preacher says
a carpenter fixed things
once for all.

Emmanuel. The people
get their hands on Him.

V: Mr. and Mrs. Trask

He's seen the type enough before:
the country pair at modest best
taking a portrait for posterity.
Between them they can dance,
mend a pump, kill a hog,
or treat the croup. Beyond that, though,
he sees the man's slight shake
–mustard gas–and his ring
finger's missing joint–sawmill.
His wife was pretty once
and probably likes Brahms or Keats.
For all their common memories
both occupy a sovereign space
and side by side negotiate.

VI: Times

Then he caught a chill
and labored on
to catch his death.

Twenty years with Robert,
forty more without.

She'll leave the mountain
with its sumac trails
and sudden falls
for some college town
with plays and picture shows.

She'll be a widow
at a glass display
or reference desk.

By luck or grace
her firstborn fighting
among islands
will live to make
the story branch.

The times are one way
so long, then something else.

Twenty years with Robert,
forty more without.*

Ozark Yarn

In a rocky, sun-pressed land,
a place of mountain reverence
and vines in valley meadow
stocked with horse, goat, and sow,
men named Homer and Virgil
gradually break their backs,
wanting no other life
less rich in struggle and lore,
told and retold on porches
to the drift of easy smoke
and casually plucked strings.

There's the time Euless Sutter,
egged on by foolhardy cohorts,
three sheets to the wind,
undertook to adorn the horns
of Taney's bull with boots.
He might've shod the beast, had he
not also tried to tie the laces.
Leviathan awoke, tossing and near
trampling the man. His rear guard
threw beer cans for distraction,
allowing him to clear the fence.
Then the rowdies marched on
to One Eye's for refueling,
laying cash on the stump,
sole honor code they observed.

Next stop, Charlie Grimes' shack,
to ogle his young bride in what
the French call her undress.

Ravished by beauty, Bo Nash
either turned a pillar of salt
(redeemed by the girl's tears)
or got that pocky look from
Charlie's double blast of such.
His comrades gave him up for
lost in their fierce skedaddle.
Swiping a canoe, they went over
Little Bear Falls in the dark
and floated ashore downstream.
Out front of Meeks Grocery
Ned Polk then got his arm stuck
fishing for a free moon pie.
Euless set out for lube or tools
but disremembered his mission
and got to joyriding instead
in a fandangled carnival truck,
playing "Turkey in the Straw"
to his very doorstep where
his overworn wife gave him
twelve distinct kinds of hell.

'Yep,' Homer sums, 'that she did,'
winding Virgil up in his turn.

Eureka

A light flocking at first under heavy promotion,
though its therapeutic springs couldn't compete
with their thermal alternatives down south
(an engineered lake later coming to the rescue).
A place of crazy-quilt passions taken
to the hills, as if flat, pragmatic lowlands
never could afford a higher view.
Veer off the two-lane snaking through
a long commercial corridor of Swiss-Bavarian conceits
and you'll get warmer, feeling the squeeze
of a more original district clad in stone,
clinging to the sides of a natural basin.
The shops are stocked with local art
you picture streaming from sunlit studios
in those Victorian cottages tucked helter
skelter along steep lane ledges. Trace the strata:
public-works comrades from the thirties,
that shaggy folkways tribe another thirty years on,
then their offspring rallied under the rainbow.
Don't book lovefest tickets just yet though.
Bible Land, LLC, has staked its local claim.
Tit: *Repent, sinners. His arm can raise or smite.*
Tat: *Why not raze that ghastly seven-story idol.*
Instead, head west of town for calmer resolution.
In a chapel of fieldstone, timber, and glass
let all that restores from high and low wash over you.*

Refugees from Atlantis
Wash Ashore in Northwest Arkansas

—after Chihuly's
Fiori Boat

Somehow they've commandeered a skiff,
braved the billows, the flotillas of plastic
so repugnant to them.

They've packed their little boat
stem to stern, determined to leave
none behind.

Having to be their own oars,
they've worked tendril lengths like cilia,
if less synchronized.

Sea birds have bombed them,
liking bright, multihued targets,
but sudden squalls

have rinsed them clean. Being what
they are, they resist that lumping insult
the great unwashed.

Taunts will still be flung—
alembic ass, hydra neck—
only to slide

off their smooth surfaces. They've not
survived a cataclysmic sea change
to give up now.

Invasive species they may be,
but consider all they have to offer:
riots of color,

relief from suburban malaise.
Having beached far inland, they'll soon
establish a footprint

colonizing highway medians and squatting
in bank lobbies. Children in cars
will count them,

men with shotguns declare open season.
They'll not be easily uprooted, though.
And as seas rise,

we may need them to bolster spreading
wetlands, even serve in a pinch
as flotation devices.*

Along Route 223

They used to blight the roadside,
but not so much these days.
One, in Texas, occupied an old drive-in,
as if, after the very last show, the cars
sighed and simply stayed put.

Here now, just south of Missouri,
by a stretch so new or negligible
it lacks a single guiding line,
a herd of junked beaters
pasture behind barbed wire.
Someone must rejoice there's somewhere
he can score a replacement hood
for a '73 Gran Torino, complete with
rust patina at no extra charge.

A few miles further on, look,
the final resting place for riding mowers,
at peace finally in long grass.

There could be a motif in the works,
like a sudden clutch of antique stores
midway between distant villages.

Logic suggests next a dirt bike dirt nap,
their tanks drained of mischief,
orphaned outboards high and dry,
ATVs past trespassing, go-carts gone kaput.

An instance perhaps of rural moralizing:
how all fast tracks leave us in the dust.

Outside Mountain View

Teeth clenched, kidneys floating,
I spot sudden relief after miles
of tortuous up-hill, down-hollow driving.
In my extremity I am almost ready
to forgive those British blokes
for mucking up the Gulf.
But what's this? Nary a pump
despite the roadside three-grade pricing.
It's now a different green come
to the rescue: a Green, Green
Grass of Home dispensary.
I'd need a special medical ID
just to get in the door.
And if I did, and if they had
facilities for customers, would I feel
obliged to buy something afterward?
I forget whether Arkansas law
even allows suffused candy bars,
or colas that harken back to origins.
No, best not think of liquids.
Just leave this inconvenience store
in the rearview and press on,
press on for greener pastures.

A Psalm of Ed

Praise the Lord upon the circular saw;
praise Him upon the door spring.

Make the strings sound upon the hambone;
make them twang upon the aerosol can.

Sing to the Lord a new song;
pluck Him a hymn from the hollow.

Plead not poverty, a pocketful of lint;
there are tools at hand: grasp them.

For the Lord abhors waste, and scorns those
who discard the good as of no worth.

His will is salvage, the saving of scraps
from the heap, the jarring made tuneable.

Have faith in God! He will not detest
the work of honest hands, however rough.

Let the sycamore and tin pot accord;
let the feral hog dance with the barn owl.

The wilderness will give up its harmony,
and the rocky places their freshets.

So be glad with the gladness of morning;
be still, for He whispers by night.*

Gayne Preller Takes Stock

My Hugo tried so many ways to fit
both here and up above: frontiersman decked
in squirrel bandolier, photographer,
fixer of guns, watches, painter of shells.
And when, during the war, churchgoing souls
turned cool toward the German among them,
he blazed fresh trails beyond this realm of dust,
true to his guiding sight of fire from ice.
How could a Kentucky gal not marry
a man like him? We took to the water;
I took to pictures, luring sitters all
along the river along of our sign:
a buxom woman astride a black bear.
We didn't play color favorites neither—
a black-and-white business, as Hugo said.
And when we'd gone as far as Arkansas,
upstream we turned, scouting the mighty White.
These rivers give and steal, you see, not just
in flow or flood, but lifeblood at the heart.
This here's our boys with strings of gigged bullfrogs,
and that lad there weighing the terrapin,
that's Victor—second Victor. First, you ask?
Well, he's the taken one, or one of them.
How many Mas and Pas have just lost track,
thinking the other kept an eagle eye?
We found him floating right beside the plank.
I aim to number blessings, but it's hard.
So then we moved ashore, and set up shop
in our catalog-ordered house of doors.
The years were mainly good, mainly a time

of prospects, the hungry thirties aside.
Course, we always had wood and stream for food,
so never felt the pinch as much as most,
and casting round came natural to us.
Victor went on to do TV repair,
like us, all-fired to bring the latest thing
in pictures here to common country folk.
But Max, poor boy, his mind swung slowly shut
after that day he shot the local drunk
for robbery and assault upon Hugo.
I try to reckon it, make it come clear,
the gains and losses, all those many doors
that open, sometimes slamming closed. You're kind
to let me rattle on. It's a plain gift,
the knack some have for finding interest.

Insider

While his friend makes cursive shapes with his fly line
he stands downstream in the shallows letting minnows

nibble his toes. It seems only fair, even if all but one
of the catches is released (for river-to-table authenticity).

The glint of light on water dazzles. He could give it
his whole mind had he a mind to surrender completely.

That and the purling could make absolute claims
if he let them. Then where would he be? Right off

the map, right off the clock, except for the sense
of sun countering crisp air and crisper stream.

For true outdoorsmen the hunt, the casting must be
a partial pretext, justifying just this immersion.

Bankside he thinks of books he should have brought:
The Compleat Angler, Trout Fishing in America.

Before he freckles, he'd better retreat to the porch
with its overhead fans and stack of bluegrass.

But then, there's that blackberry bush his friend praised.
Dragonflies copter around him. *Come, come, come.*

Downsizing

If he were given to large gestures, he would say
Damn the homeowners association, damn the city codes
and turn his yard into a meadow for the vanishing.
Out with carpetlike zoysia, in with milkweed
for Monarchs on their wing-wearing migration.
And for collapsing colonies, forget-me-nots by way
of apology for all the negligence to date.
He'd go walking knee-deep in flutter and buzz,
trailing palms across the sway of sweet alyssum,
his tabby's tail just detectable among orange poppies.

Then again, a more defined space,
say, six by nine, with split-
rail fence for border, might suffice.
Plenty room for purple heather,
blue flax, and the bonanza
of hues lavendered with scent.
Air traffic would be heavy,
like Denver at Christmas.

At day's end he sows
a tight circle of
coneflowers, coreopsis,
baby's breath and hyssop
in a recycled
whiskey barrel,
breaks ground for
his butterfly bistro,
bee bar.

The Striper

In the large, empty lot he steers a machine
like a mower with a tank of white paint,

retracing faded lines on weather-worn blacktop,
asserting definition and the wisdom of limits.

Passersby might assume a meticulous childhood
of coloring books like stained-glass cathedrals,

but they'd be wrong. All that butterfly
and rainbow business he left to girls.

Strict play within chalked shapes on grass
also failed to draw his aimless energies.

With ten years of schooling he's racked up
a mess of low-wage jobs, a broken marriage,

a pedestrian slate of misdemeanors,
and a sense of happiness as stolen goods.

Life always exacts payback—he knows that now—
taxing sin and charging sky-high interest.

Punishment matches crime: for years of drinking,
drugging, skirt chasing, he gets to spend whole days

toeing, walking, hell, laying down the damn line.

Exegesis

Not your standard cardboard hard-luck story
but a stencilled sandwich-board revelation
on a lanky black man with a white dummy
hanging from his neck. The sunshade makes sense;
that megaphone, though: whose mouth is it for?
There's a recessive metaphor at work here
involving vessels, mouthpieces, controlling hands;
it's a street performance in hermeneutics
more demanding than the water-from-sand act
or the guy who folds himself into a small box.
Notice how the text rides his back:

> SENSE 2000 FED ON HIDDEN MANNA
> AND NAMED ANEW IN THE WHITE STONE.
> FLASH: TRUST NOT IN RAYGONS AND
> MIDEAST BURNING BUSHES! ONLY ONE
> GATED COMUNEITY JERUSALEM HIGHTS.
> 12 FOUNDATIONS (REV. 21: 19-20). LOTS
> GOING FAST. ADMISSION PRICE RIGHT-
> OUSNESS, THE BLOOD WITH BLEACHING
> KRYSTALS. RENOUNS FALSE SEALS.
> TURN OFF A/C. ROLL DOWN WINDOWS.
> OPEN TO THE KNOCKING (REV. 3:20).
> HEAT WILL PASS (FOR SOME!). REJOICE.
> GREAT TRADE-IN. CHRISTOPRAISES
> FOR SINNOMAN.

Is this a Gulf War vet turning tables on the Man?
And the spoken parts, do they gloss the placard
or spin it like some bizarre McCarthy hypertext?
If so, he do the Lord in different voices.

To cut the babel of radios, cell phones, and engines
that megaphone has to ventriloquize keenly.
Then the timing of his red-light spiel must be
stand-up sharp to catch the muzzy sheep.
It all seems too much to ask, a camel squeeze.
As the light changes, the pharmacy sign announces
it's 92° at 4:47, and sleep aids are on sale.

County Museum

Not much of a county, more a matter of rice and soybeans
than people, who decamp year by year for higher ground.

It's never been easy. A jackleg diorama with a broken light
shows a Civil War skirmish that demolished the first county seat.

Then in the twenties a double hit: first a twister went
window shopping down Main Street; when that damage was fixed,

a flood floated all merchandise, furniture, and boats alike.
In the decades since, first passenger, then freight trains stopped

coming through town. A hundred yards or so of track remains.
They just managed to save the depot, now home to the museum

and chamber of commerce. It's a tribute to tenacity,
the way the legendary local doc kept making house calls

into his late eighties. They've preserved his office, staged it
along with scenes from schoolroom, bank, bakery, and chapel.

When called, their young have served—witness the doughboy
and GI gear—but mostly they kept the farms and silos going.

If you count neighboring delta, they've also shared homegrown
talent with the world—mainly blues endemic to these parts,

but also that piano-pounding yelp of Saturday-night release,
repented next morning in soulful pleas for grace.

Threads

We picture them in a circle piecing patterns
of stars or geometric blossoms,
arranging the scraps of past seasons
into a cover against the year's bottoming.

Their needles prick and stitch, prick and stitch,
all the while they speak of husbands, children,
household tasks, and prizes at the county fair.

A century on, some grace not beds but
museum walls. There's Log Cabin,
a tribute in pink to nursery rhymes,
Old Glory waving in tufted strips.

What fixes me though came singlehanded
from Camden circa 1900, called Lily Quilt
though a rugged phalanx of crosses.

This is how time gets stitched, the fabric
adorned with scarcely traceable designs
encompassing the most disparate swatches of life.

Asia Cummings Shed blankets me
with her making, and I in turn now
extend neighborly acquaintance to you.*

Elaine

Not a woman,
a fought-over woman,

a fought-over woman
in a juke joint,

a Delta juke joint
with a kerosene pail,

a tipped pail that sets
the juke joint afire,

a fire that near burns
a bluesman's guitar,

a Delta blues guitar
now named for a woman.

No, not that, but
blue, dark Delta blue,

spilling from a church,
a flash-point church,

spilling into fields,
hard, killing fields,

Delta fields that holler,
holler blue-black murder

to deaf air about town,
a town named Elaine.*

Imitation of Christ

The kid on the highway shoulder
is dragging a cross through the gravel,
trailed by a pink golf cart.
Evangelical newsmaking probably,
or penance for adolescent sin.
He looks sincerely prayerful:
Jesus, don't let me die
like a locust on a rig grill.

Some pleas must be answered,
because next day the state police
have collared the little procession.
No official hand washing this time.
End of the line on the road to
the road to Damascus, Arkansas.

IQ Zoo

Who could resist Bandit the All-Net Raccoon,
or the plunking of Professor Long Hare?
Four bits got you safecracking squirrels,
Rosie the Multiplying Pig, and our star attraction,
a hen who'd whipped B. F. Skinner at tic-tac-toe.
It was easy to mistake us, though, for just another
Spa City amusement like miniature golf
or roadside funland with carousel and pony ride.
What other outfit covertly trained pigeons
to guide missiles? Dolphins in our program
graduated to tracking enemy subs.
Pure *Strangelove* stuff. Behaviorism's slam dunk.
If the Bay of Pigs had included a couple of
our porkers, Fidel's days would've been numbered.
Human intelligence has its place, but on the ground
you won't find a dog second-guessing its nose,
or barking up some planted decoy of a tree.
And when all the documents are declassified,
the public will learn that even as Mr. Gorbachev
was being exhorted to tear down that wall,
our moles were already on the job.*

A Day at the Races

It's because I treat the thing as
a beauty pageant, and the prettiest horses
seldom win, unlike the human scramble.
Wash down those hapless two-buck bets
with stacked roast beef and beer.

Today there's plenty unsuccess to go around.
The young trumpeter stumbles repeatedly on
the rapid-fire triplets of "First Call,"
reveille for runners bellying to the gate.

And they're off . . .
churning earth at full gallop,
innocent of the wagers they carry,
that phantom interest weightier than jockeys.

If I had a thoroughbred,
I'd name it Fifth of Forth,
just to muddy the waters,
or maybe Snowball's Chance, a shoo-in
for the Triple Crown, or else
king of the essential also-rans,
the ones perpetually lost in the pack,
missing pay dirt, shouldering the
odds-on favorite (who may only show).*

Ouachita Wonderland

A light in the darkness,
or rather, four million of them

strung to show the way,
enthrall, the old draw
of color and shine.

And the strains that urge Peace,
urge Joy,
to cap a year short on both.

Even the barest tree dazzles
sketched in radiance.

Pass through a wreathed arbor

to a neon pond
where a frog prince flicks
lightning bugs with red tongue

as eagle-sized butterflies flit
among glazed flowers,
this wired garden eclipsing
the real one.

It's the holiday spirit
in overdrive,

king spruce mantled with
emerald and ruby bands,

a full-press charm putsch,

kids swarming the next-stop-
anywhere express.

Still, you're in no mood
to resist,

lulled with hot chocolate,

glamoured by the blue
fairy glen.

Time enough to be scorched
by day's cold bulb.*

Arkansas

It comes home to us, the name's core:
                              downriver.
Because it raises its head a thousand
miles northwest, among red rocks and lead,
then winds through two more states before
reaching here, finally paying its tribute
of waters to the nation's spinal flow.
Along the way it collects a whole region's
rainfall; well, it and the interrupters
with their pent-up pleasure lakes.
Flood control is just that, controlled
flooding, measured by the gallon, cubic foot,
measured damage that damages least,
depending, though, on the earthen dams
downstream, levees gnawed by flood-stage
currents until here and there one breaches,
turning fields and towns into wading pools.

We'll all be downstream people soon
enough, south of our crying carelessness,
cursing our former upstream selves
for hogging, abusing, off-kiltering
what seemed naturally gyroscopic.
Maybe the new spin will show
the spoiler despoiled, forced into
better channels, if good and lucky
brought around to the cycles that sustain.*

Thereabouts

ABC of Loss

—after Pinsky

A bare coffin,
deal.

Ethan, five.

Grief hoarsens
into jarring keys:

Lift. . . .

Mourning neighbors,
only parent.

Quicken. . . .

Registry signed
the usual
variant way:

X

Yearning's
zero.

Brown Study in Blue and Gray

—Shiloh

Among orchards they gathered to paint the sky
>   Conscious of braver colors
To be streaked and dashed in passionate bursts
>   Blending as they hovered.
So long from public square and country porch
>   The azure seemed unremitting
As if their skies were not of a piece with
>   The span of detailed living.
So they drafted their beasts to haul iron and wood
>   For scaffolding to the sky
Setting their sights on incomparable feats
>   Of staunch derring-do-or-die.
In the heat of contention the peach blossoms showered
>   And droves stooped low to drink
In poses that struck them as unbecoming
>   For shavers still in the pink.

Natchez

She wants to see the observation room
Up top but can't. Always the velvet rope
Blocking the spiral stair or upper floor
Or cozy nook with storybook stained glass.
It's strange such things should aggravate this late.
Maybe she's just nettled to be rushed through
The his and her parlors mirrored ten deep.
Such wealth: Italian mantels, chandeliers
Of heavy bronze in fantastic detail,
All tinged of course with old plantation guilt.
Their tour guide pauses, tells a maid, Clarice,
To close some door, the tone a touch regal.
Not that relations win a prize back home,
The interstate almost a color line.
Though gateway west, her city neighbors south.
A few hundred miles upriver from here,
She thinks, then pictures twin golden arches
And moored casinos lining tourist shores.
That brings the sudden thought she knows little
About Lewis and Clark. Her brain does leap.
In fact, she must confess a jumpy streak
For some months now, an urge to have her way.
When Bill with customary cool and calm
Shot down her proffered Bourbon Street romance
By citing rates of crime and hotel rooms,
She nearly shut her mind against his plan:
The waterworks outside Vicksburg for him,
And this for her. But thirty years' assent
To engineer's logic is hard to break.

"Well, Dot, can't say you're not enjoying it.

The carriage-house restaurant out back will do
For lunch; the sandwiches are moderate.
Unless you want . . ."
                              No, moderate is fine.
About her mood, however, he has erred.
It's not just pleasure; pain is in it too,
Or stirrings like it. Why does she respond
So strongly to this gone domestic world
Of twelve-foot ceilings, silk, and teaster beds?
Beneath a paddle fan for shooing flies
There once was table talk about a dance
Or yellow fever. And that handsome boy
Portrayed in oils: she reads he grew to be
A banker, married, died at twenty-eight.
She must try again to persuade her son
Not to put off having children too long.
On this at least she and his wife agree.

                    * * *

The afternoon works long at building heat.
They stroll magnolia shade admiring lawns,
Exchanging bits of talk. She'd like to try
A horse-drawn carriage, just the kind of thing
That runs against her husband's temperament.
An old black man requests money for food.
She reaches for her purse, but Bill stops her,
Asserting after, chicken means liquor.

                    * * *

They tour next through a Greek Revival house,

Still occupied, and packed with bric-a-brac
Of generations. Teddy bears in chairs
Hold perpetual council in the nursery.
A massive dining-room cabinet displays
Fine china hand-painted by Audubon.
She pauses, though, before a Kodachrome
Of family fun around a pool. Out back
She finds a concrete hole filling with leaves.
It comes to her when she was young they closed
The pools and shows in fear of polio.
Her mother tried so hard those summer months
To keep her entertained.
                              Bill wanders out
At length and spots a woman on a bench
Under a live-oak tree two centuries old.
The sunlight gently bathes her face and hands.

* * *

Bookstores look right decked in Victorian.
While Bill flips through the how-to magazines
She combs a sale on coffee-table stock.
The glossy Faberge she'd like to have,
But fifty dollars seems extravagant.
In self-debate she casts a vacant glance
Upon a wall of classic novels, things
She read in school but very seldom since.
Somehow it seems remiss of her, as if
Quite small concerns had crowded out the large.
Where to begin? And then she chooses one
Whose title strikes her: *Great Expectations.*

* * *

The word is not to miss the octagon
Pagoda house, a tour de force of wealth
Grown fanciful. They're not disappointed.
Her husband marks the clever use of pipes
To heat and cool. That just the basement floor
Was furnished when the War stopped work for good
Impresses her, the upper levels less
And less complete up to the onion dome.
Some relative led Union troops onto
A major Pennsylvania battlefield.
Not Gettysburg, she thinks; it starts with A.
Or was it Maryland? The dome can't say.
If only memory weren't so like a sieve.

* * *

Locals call it dining under the hill,
A river bluff commercial at its base.
She scans the softening light as Bill explains
The benefits of side air bags in cars.
When ordering she almost takes pork chops,
But checks herself and goes with blackened shrimp.
A margarita too. Bill cocks a brow
Then joins her with an untried German beer.
Over her drink she feels how hard it is
To disappear as if one never lived.

* * *

A new day lands them at the riverboats.
They plan to stroll the *Delta's* deck before
Leaving, but learn just passengers can board.
So Bill hikes up the hill to fetch the car
And Dot remains to mull her stark dismay,
Which finds simple relief as she glides past
The occupied ramp-wallah, sure as sure
This once she'll taste the fruit of stolen joy.
Both boat and river sparkle in the sun
To jingling sounds she comes to recognize
As slot machines dispensing happiness
Inside the parlor where luck has steered her,
The roll of coins she keeps for tolls at hand.
If nothing else, she'll get her money's worth
Of bells and whistles. Dropping ten coins fast,
She figures to be through in no time flat,
Then wins a round, applauded by the boat's
Resounding horn. The odds reclaim her gains
Until the final quarter buys a spin
Of LEMON-CHERRY-LEMON. Easy go.
Retreating toward the ramp, she finds a gulf
Expanding wide between herself and Bill,
Who signals vainly from the shore. Instead
Of panic, wry acceptance seizes her
And she waves back, shrugging, then gestures south.
He is dependable; she counts on him
To be there when she docks at New Orleans.
This new chapter may stymie him at first,
But Dorothy Wheeler's book is not yet closed.
She goes the way the muddy river leads,
Foreseeing deeper waters worth their salt.

Cabin Fever

"The angels shorely are a-comin' to fetch me,"
the boy vamped, recruiting the dove flutter
outside the window. "Afore I go"—and here
he managed a consumptive rattle—
"I want to give all of ya'll"—namely,
his younger brother, older sister, cousin,
and fleabit hound—"a beeootiful curl
to treasure the rest of your bawn days."
So saying, he took a pair of garden shears
and severed strands of lemony yarn
from the Raggedy Ann fright wig on his noggin.

The inspiration for this burlesque pietà—
Little Eva's farewell to her loved ones—
he'd scented somehow through that innate
genius for mockery now ripe in its tenth year.

Milking the bathos with eye rolls, spasms
that caused Beauregard to snap for his share,
and cooing sighs designed to make PJ
pee himself with laughter, this lapsing cherub
worked the room like a shameless vaudevillean.
Sister resisted the farcical blandishments
with indifferent success, while cousin Bailey
offered prompts that largely went ignored.

Drawn by the hubbub, Mrs. Devereux collared
her budding John Wilkes by the yellow scruff
and gave him a willow-switch what-for,
not because he'd pilloried some carpetbagging
novel, but for wasting her canary stock

and flirting with derisive irreligion,
like those fleering children eaten by a bear.

Young master Jack sulked briefly that
his art should be so grievously traduced,
then hit upon a scheme to soothe the satiric
soul that called for an ancestral portrait,
a cedar duck call, rope on a pulley,
and his father's favorite billiards cue.

Moreover, he'd recast the audience, improve its tone.*

Sci-Fi in Midsummer South

The bug that bit Weldon Maxwell may have dwelt
between the pages of a Philip K. Dick novel
picked almost at random from the stacks of paperbacks
lining the walls of Blue Tick Used Books.
So Weldon's mother was possibly right in claiming
that someday the kinds of books he read (she called it trash)
would warp his sense of what's real for good.
Certain others hold that Weldon got notions
from staring at the distant behavior of railroad tracks,
but whatever the cause his case has been contagious.
Gramaw Stuckey was the first to defend the boy,
saying that she herself often had powerful
strange thoughts while making quilts or pie crusts
which she just had to keep to herself.
Talk about alternate worlds and time-switching
soon loaded the grapevine; beneath the sign
of the winged, red horse infected old-timers
tangled family trees more thoroughly than ever.
By this stage peculiar markings had appeared
under the town name on the water tower
and the water itself tasted different to most.
Meanwhile at the downtown movie house
Weldon was taking advantage of his job as usher
to distribute pairs of 4-D glasses, thereby
giving the westerns a whole new dimension.
Outsiders have noticed a change in the locals,
that they are more wary of outsiders these days.
This year's town fair went unannounced at large
and rumor has it that the first-place entry
in the produce division was an unidentified because

unearthly vegetable submitted by Eb Dawson.
Yet to make the county gossip circuit is
report of a new twist on an old fair event:
the toad jump, now revamped into toad croquet.
The wickets of course are Weldon's doing.
Coaxed to jump through one hoop, the toad
comes sailing or flopping through another somewhere
else on the playing field; there is a winning pattern
to be discovered or chanced upon by man or toad.
So far all the newfangledness has been taken
in stride by the townsfolk, and should the outside
world get to prying too much into their business,
they expect the trail could get to branching so fast
that any snoop would wind up chasing his tail.
Gramaw Stuckey speaks for all when she says
it's unneighborly to meddle in the affairs of good plain folk.

Original Sin

He's not buying it.
Eating an apple,
even a forbidden one,
couldn't mean such
big trouble for them
and their kids
and then their kids
even down to himself.

No, they must have
done something
so *original*,
so unthought of,
that God's jaw
dropped in disbelief.

He knows such things
happen, not often,
kept secret by adults
in whispers and hints.

He's put his mind
to it, looking
like he's praying,
such a whopper
that first one
would seem plain
pathetic, a bunt.

It's hard, though,
and all he's got

is palming money
from the brass plate
for cherry bombs
to blow the wings
off graveyard cherubs.

Maybe he doesn't have
what it takes
to be legendary bad.
Maybe he's doomed
to take his place
among the chosen,
forever singing hymns
to Miz Eugenia's
wheezy spinster organ
in clip-on tie
and stiff dress shoes,
no chance in heck
to scuff up his soul.

Goat

Two rows of
wooden chairs
back to back
extend the length
of the fellowship hall.
A loop of people
like a bicycle chain
goes down each side.
The child understands
when the music stops
he must quickly sit
because there are not
enough chairs for all.
Being quite young,
and probably between
chairs at the moment
for action,
he finds himself
the last one standing,
hence the first one out.
No room at the inn
for him. Devastated,
he dissolves in tears.
There is consolation,
a page to color
with Jesus feeding
the five thousand.
But he doesn't want
that, he wants a chair,
to be still in the game,

not the one regarded
with relief and pity
by the survivors.
That they will follow
in defeat hardly touches
his exclusive grief.
Incapable of metaphor,
of seeing past
the present catastrophe,
he chokes on the pain,
as on something
too large to swallow,
impossible to stomach.

Forecast

On this eve of twisters
the tag-team weathermen
speak of wall clouds,
hook echoes, rotation,
point out ominous bulges
in the ragged stormline.
Fronts primed for funnels
stress, excite them.
They are ready, display
the latest tracking gear
precise to street level,
dramatize the peril
from block to block,
in coming seasons maybe
house to menaced house:
"Timmy Hall of 314 Elm,
get away from the window.
We know you're hypnotized
by the swaying cobra
of dirt-darkened wind
vacuuming your town,
a terror more horrendous
than any you've dreamed.
At eight years old
it's your first glimpse
of the godlike–dreadful,
magnificent, capricious–
sparing the liquor store,
smashing the daycare.
Tear yourself away now,

run for the bathroom
and dive in the tub.
You have memories there,
happy ones, though they
and every childhood thing
will soon take flight
for the next county,
leaving you shaken, grazed,
beneath clearing skies
whose shelter of blue
like all those below
you'll never quite trust."

Indian Summer

Central Florida, 1971, a middling
subdivision of concrete-block
houses with screened porches for
grilling and daiquiri sipping.
Kids find their cool
at the community pool,
hanging around the aquamarine
clubhouse to the beat of
hormones and "Indian Reservation."
Grinning, boys note budding girls
but still prefer pinball to
active pursuit. Outside they clown
or show off on the boards,
lifeguards whistling wildest
savages from the drink.
No swimming really, just splashing,
dunking, Marco Polo searches:
youngsters' last hurrah of
horseplay in the shallow end.

Caving

A cold draft marks the opening,
straight and low into the hillside.
Daylight just reaches the ledge above
a ball-and-breast-gripping stream,
occasion for archly sexist echoes
among spelunkers in deep together.
Here no brochures, no elevator to
a concrete path with guardrail
through fantasia scapes of flow
stone, stalactite and stalagmite, all
lit with colored floods; rather,
flashlights peer quizzically in crisscross,
flicking the likelihood of wedged
foot, bruised hip, and starry vision.
The ceiling lowers, leaving inches
of breath for crouched wading.
Take heart, our guide assures us,
no underwater stretches here, just
cramped fissures, salamander crawlways,
dragon-sized chambers, smooth corridors—
all stony to fatigue and bad batteries.
To save light, rest stops are blind;
nervous voices ripple the void.
Within this massive down-under
time dilates into aeons, patient
as drops of water sculpting caverns.
Utter darkness behind and to come;
were there ever days in the sun?
Moving again, seeking entry outward,
feet hold to a gradual incline

(the stream slithered off an hour ago),
sixth sense correcting stray impulse.
Desire anticipates until the line
quivers to a certain pluck
and the straggling mole people
emerge into lichen light,
collecting for a steep climb out
a rolling country's sinkhole.

Pearl

At the very last he recalls
not how his father beat him
with a radiator hose while
his mother turned away;
not how he became
his own man at fourteen,
by nineteen somewhat less
than honorably discharged
from the rule-bound Navy;
not how close he came
to doing real time for
selling stolen cigarettes,
though if he had, he might
have been spared yet more
misadventures on the street;
not how whiskey proved
his most steady false friend
until one day he left
the gutter and city behind,
bankrolled by a bookie
who mistook him for
someone more trustworthy;
not how he spent two years
drifting as a farmhand,
drying out enough to try
another city and married life;
not how he went through
three wives and twice that
many jobs, sticking to beer
if not always sobriety;

not how only two of his five
kids will speak to him,
and the number of grandkids
remains a bit hazy;
not how of late he's wanted
to smash that imposter
returning his disgusted stare.
No, what he recalls is how
once in Macon a young man
cheered by drinking buddies
who thought well of him
bowled a perfect game.

Geraldine Page

On sleep's border the fugitive appears, innocent, casual. Eureka. Surely the calling and grid search played a part. Next morning, though, vanished. How? I rack and pummel fruitlessly. Gone, gone. Bad brain. To work: Pa–, Pa–, Pa-tri-cia Neal. No. Again: Pa . . . tri . . . No, dammit. Reset. First name old-fashioned. Gwendolyn. Florence. Hermione. Halt, only getting further afield. Opening shot of bluebonnets. Visual trumps verbal. Her face, aglow with Protestant hymns, turned toward home. Reset. Association. Author: Foote. Horton, not Shelby. Cast: son, played by John . . . Heard. Good. Avoided the Hurt-Voight trap. Young woman on bus, wholesome, not like *Risky* character. Alas, another blank. Recall unbountiful. Can do Charlize Theron, Gwyneth Paltrow, Uma Thurman with exertion. Ladies, ladies, the crush gums the mechanism. Hence, Jessica Tandy. Take Kate with you. Leave me to fret and stew over today's missing link. I could cheat, but mustn't. No shortcuts. Go the hard road.*

Texas Allows Guns
in College Classrooms

Et in Arcadia ego, y'all. The groves of academe
have been unnaturally peaceful long enough.

Down with elitist hedges. Down with monastic cloisters.
The century is twenty-one, going on nineteen.

Mesquite groves, after all: part of the endless frontier
for men and women raised on cactus and rattlers.

The campus drinking hole always wanted to be a saloon,
honky tonk making hoity-toity dance a coltish jig.

Hell with tippy-toe pointy-headed debates:
an argument's only as good as its holstered logic.

Reckon the packing professor a town sheriff:
You got anything to add, you take it outside.

The Darwin and Genesis gangs do just that,
pistol-whipping sense into each other.

No culture war worth its salt can be fought
with words alone. That's just shooting blanks.

How better to put the yee-haw back in school?
Targets produce the most measurable outcomes.

Frank Dodge, Fake Cowboy Poet, Sends His Regrets

He won't be making the Amarillo Roundup,
thanks just the same, not much caring
to be branded and ridden out of town
on a tarred sawhorse. Fact is, Frank Dodge

himself qualifies as a character, a persona.
His creator has never strung barbed wire,
never roped anything, and his cattle experience
mainly consists of managing an Arby's.

Not that he meant to perpetrate a hoax.
Schooled in Remington and Russell,
L'Amour and Zane Grey, he found his truer,
maybe previous self out among the sage.

If fate in this life has consigned him
to a ranch house in suburban hell, so be it.
He'll ride the trail, birth the foals, and tell
rodeo tales around his portable campfire.

One critic has called his work "the real deal,
redolent of sweat, dust, and prairie pathos."
All he asks is what fiction writers claim:
the right to make a world from whole cloth.

But folks will have their verse gospel pure,
straight from the journal of the poet's days,
and his skin isn't nearly leathery enough
to hang credibility from a handlebar moustache.

Lately there have been mutters and murmurs
among his peers, who call him the ghost rider.
He conducts all business by email, and even
has published work sent c/o his brother in Durango.

So what if coyotes don't serenade the moon
in Saginaw, Michigan? This mitten-state tenderfoot
haunts the bunkhouse, romances rustling chaparral.
There's tallness in the saddle on switchbacks too.

Notes

"Revelation"
Folk medicine held that bezoars, a stonelike accretion in the stomach of certain animals, could counteract poison and maladies such as rabies. A bezoar, or madstone, in an albino deer was believed especially potent. I first learned of this supposed antidote from a newspaper article by outdoors writer Keith Sutton.

The cataclysm towards poem's end is the New Madrid earthquake (or quakes) of 1811-12.

"Arkopolis"
If *Little Rock* had not won out, we would now know the capital of the Natural State as *Arkopolis*.

"Aftermath"
Though estimated casualties vary, around a thousand lives were lost when the steamboat *Sultana*, carrying Federal troops who had been prisoners of war, exploded and sank on April 27, 1865.

"Over Here"
Arkansas witnessed pockets of armed resistance to the draft in World War I. This poem focuses on the Ozarks front.

The followers of American evangelist Charles Taze Russell were known as Russellites. His version of Adventist belief contributed to the formation of the Jehovah's Witness movement.

"Sundown"
Sundown towns sought to exclude African American residents. Their money was welcome during business hours, but they themselves were expected to leave town by sunset.

"Mountain Airs"
The modern-classical composer Michael Brown has set this poem cycle to music.

"Eureka"
This piece works the east-west axis in Eureka Springs, moving from the Christ of the Ozarks statue and Great Passion Play on one edge of town to Thorncrown Chapel by E. Fay Jones on the other.

"Refugees from Atlantis Wash Ashore in Northwest Arkansas"
More specifically, this boatload of glass creatures has beached at the Crystal Bridges Museum of American Art.

"A Psalm of Ed"
A tribute to Ozarks craftsman Ed Stilley, maker of primitive guitars out of scrap materials.

"Threads"
Asia Cummings Shed's Lily Quilt, created about 1890, is on the cover of this book.

"Elaine"
The first half of the poem references the story behind B. B. King's naming his guitar Lucille. The second half recalls the Elaine race riot, or massacre, of 1919.

"IQ Zoo"
According to the *Arkansas Encyclopedia*, animal behaviorists Keller and Marian Breland operated the IQ Zoo attraction in Hot Springs between 1955 and 1990.

"A Day at the Races"
The Spa City is also the site of this poem.

"Ouachita Wonderland"
This poem refers to the Holiday Lights event at Garvan Woodland Gardens on the outskirts of Hot Springs.

"Arkansas"
The Arkansas River flooded a number of low-lying areas in the summer of 2019. Conway, where I live, experienced a near miss as the local levee eroded but just held.

"Cabin Fever"
Jack parodies Little Eva's death scene from chapter 26 of *Uncle Tom's Cabin*.

"Geraldine Page"
Page won an Oscar for Best Actress for her performance in *The Trip to Bountiful*. In the interest of full disclosure, I must admit that I finally broke down and looked up her name. The flesh isn't the only thing that's weak.

CPSIA information can be obtained
at www.ICGtesting.com
Printed in the USA
FSHW021414010420
68684FS

$15.95

James Fowler, former editor of the poetry journal *Slant*, teaches literature at the University of Central Arkansas. He has published poetry, fiction, and essays. His poems have appeared in such journals as *Cave Region Review*, *Elder Mountain, Cantos, Futures Trading Magazine, Valley Voices, Aji Magazine, Dash,* and *Westview*.

Fowler unfolds a many-sided verbal diorama of the history and culture of Arkansas and the South. Observer and participant, he combines wit, irony, acumen, empathy, and a sense of place to salvage the sacred and noble from even the most chaotic remnants of human recklessness. Fowler, like his protagonist in the title poem, absorbs regret, sorrow, guilt, and pain and translates it all into vigorous and vibrant art that humanizes the past and offers redemption.

--Phil Howerton, author of *The History of Tree Roots*, editor of *An Anthology of Ozark Literature*

ISBN 978-1-936135-89-9

golden antelope

GROWING IN
CIRCLES
Learning the rhythms of discipleship

PAUL HARCOURT